Suzuki®

FLUTE SCHOOL

Volume 9
Flute Part

CONTENTS

© 1993 Dr. Shinichi Suzuki
Sole publisher for the entire world except Japan:
Summy-Birchard, Inc.
Exclusive print rights administered by Alfred Music Publishing Co., Inc.
All rights reserved   Printed in USA

ISBN-10: 0-7579-2503-0
ISBN-13: 978-0-7579-2503-0

The Suzuki name, logo and wheel device
are trademarks of Dr. Shinichi Suzuki
used under exclusive license by Summy-Bichard, Inc.

INTRODUCTION

FOR THE STUDENT: This material is part of the worldwide Suzuki Method® of teaching. The companion recording should be used along with this publication. In addition, there are piano accompaniment books that go along with this material.

FOR THE TEACHER: In order to be an effective Suzuki teacher, ongoing education is encouraged. Each regional Suzuki association provides teacher development for its membership via conferences, institutes, short-term and long-term programs. In order to remain current, you are encouraged to become a member of your regional Suzuki association, and, if not already included, the International Suzuki Association.

FOR THE PARENT: Credentials are essential for any Suzuki teacher you choose. We recommend you ask your teacher for his or her credentials, especially those related to training in the Suzuki Method®. The Suzuki Method® experience should foster a positive relationship among the teacher, parent and child. Choosing the right teacher is of utmost importance.

To obtain more information about the Suzuki Association in your region, please contact:

International Suzuki Association
www.internationalsuzuki.org

Attack Exercises in lower register

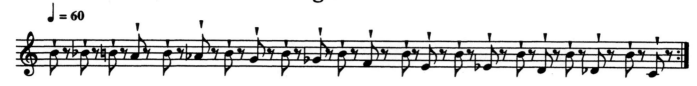

° Relax the lips except in the center where muscles should be slightly tensed horizontally while keeping the jaw a little in a relaxed position.

° Attack with the short air friction noise, with low air pressure behind the lower lip, vibrating well in the mouth.

Attack Exercises in middle and high register

° Attack with the same short air friction noise, with more air pressure behind the lower lip, vibrating well in the mouth.

Articulation Exercises

Accent the 1st note of the four, clearly articulating the last 2 detached with a single tongue movement.

Clearly accent the 1st note, broadening the 3 slurred notes, but articulating the last.

Accent the 1st note, make it distinctly clear from the 3 slurred notes by making it short and clearly lengthen the 3 slurred notes so as to keep the 4 notes quite equal.

Accent the 1st of the 2 slurred notes and diminish the second but do not let it go; diminishing gives lightness without inequality.

♩ = 72 *Reprise a' l'octave*

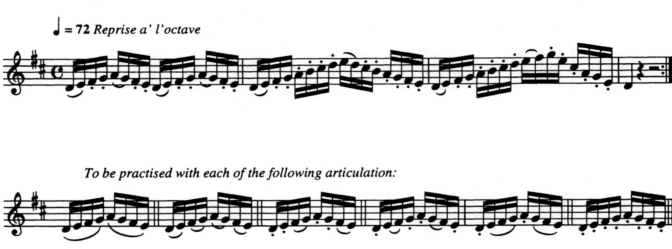

To be practised with each of the following articulation:

♩ = 72 *Reprise a' l'octave*

To be practised with each of the following articulations

Trill Exercises

Preparatory Exercises

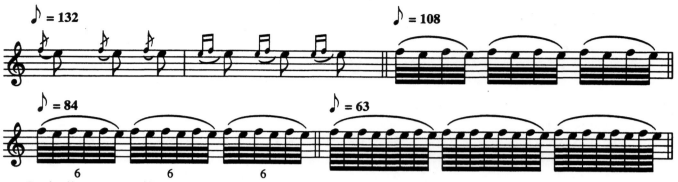

Basically start all trills on the higher note and on the beat. Long trill is a kind of fingering vibrato, and short trill is a kind of accent.

Ex.

○ Thrust your jaw downward.

○ Take care of the lip condition and air pressure.

○ Fingers should be well arched.

○ Start with good attack, reverberating well in the mouth and throat.

1 CONCERTO IN D MAJOR

フルート協奏曲 第2番

W.A. MOZART
KV314
Revised by T. Takahashi

10

12

16

Cadenza (Donjon)